TARA AND MICHELLE
THE ROAD TO GOLD

TARA AND MICHELLE
THE ROAD TO GOLD

By Wendy Daly

Random House 🏠 New York

All rights reserved under International and Pan-American Copyright Convention. Published in the United States by Random House, Inc., New York, and simultaneously in Canada by Random House of Canada Limited, Toronto.

http://www.randomhouse.com

Library of Congress Catalog Card Number: 97-066957
ISBN: 0-679-88930-2
R.L.: 4.0

Printed in the United States of America

10 9 8 7 6 5 4 3 2

To my mother, Betty Santley Healy

CONTENTS

Introduction   1

MICHELLE

1. Nerds, Rental Skates, and an Ice Castle   12
2. A Sneaky Move   22
3. The '94 Olympics—Almost   30
4. Makeup and Medals   41

TARA

5. Little Skates, Big Ambitions   54
6. A Family Divided   60
7. "Short But Good"   70
8. "Leapin' Lipinski!"   78

TARA AND MICHELLE

9. Thrills and Spills   86
10. The Road to the Worlds   94
11. The Youngest Champion   98
12. Beyond the Rink   107
    Olympic Gold Medalists   115
    Michelle Kwan Time Line   116
    Tara Lipinski Time Line   118

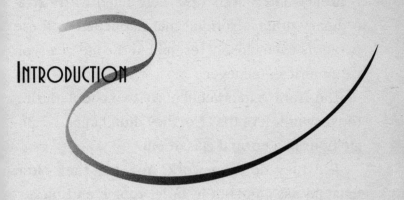

INTRODUCTION

Think back to the winter of 1997. Do you remember anything special that happened in your life during February and March? You probably went to school during the week. Most likely, you did your homework, enjoyed some after-school activities, and spent time with your family and friends. Maybe you played sports or had some fun sleepovers on the weekends. Or maybe you can't remember anything in particular about that time—you just know that your life went on as usual.

But for fourteen-year-old Tara Lipinski and

sixteen-year-old Michelle Kwan, the months of February and March 1997 were filled with extraordinary drama. Nothing that happened to these two girls even closely resembled the life of a typical American teenager.

Did Tara and Michelle go to school during those winter months? No, they didn't spend a single hour in a normal classroom.

Did they do homework? Yes, but they often finished assignments in hotel rooms and on airplanes and E-mailed them back to their private tutors.

Did Tara and Michelle have time for normal after-school activities? No, not when they were spending three or four hours every day at a cold skating rink, training on the ice with their coaches. Not when they were being interviewed by reporters. And certainly not when they were traveling around the globe, performing in exhibitions and competing against the best figure skaters in the world.

Tara and Michelle took part in three major skating competitions during the winter of 1997.

Michelle was the more experienced skater, and she was expected to win all three events. But something completely unexpected happened at one competition—the United States Figure Skating Championships in Nashville, Tennessee.

Wearing an elaborate costume, Michelle was on the ice, performing the same routine that had earned her first-place awards all winter in other competitions. One moment she was twirling through the air in a difficult jump called a triple toe loop. The next moment she was falling hard onto the ice. She scrambled to her feet and kept skating, the way her coach had taught her. But then she panicked and fell again.

This was very unusual for Michelle. She had skated almost perfectly all season. She had won this same national competition just the year before. She had won the world championship, too. Michelle Kwan was already considered to be America's best hope for a gold medal at the 1998 Winter Olympics in Nagano, Japan.

As Michelle struggled on the ice, Tara Lipinski was waiting to skate next. Michelle Kwan was one of Tara's idols. Tara looked up to Michelle, and not just because Michelle was five feet two inches, while she was only four feet eight inches. Tara admired Michelle's grace and style on the ice.

Suddenly, Tara realized she might have a chance to beat Michelle in a competition. But Tara refused to let herself think about that as she glided onto the ice to skate her program. She knew that she needed to focus all of her attention on her own performance. She only hoped that, for the next four minutes, she could skate as well as she had in practice all week.

Music from the movie *Sense and Sensibility* filled the packed Nashville Arena. That was Tara's cue to begin. She started off strongly, picking up the speed she needed for her first triple jump. A smile lit up her face after she executed the jump perfectly. And she kept on smiling as she landed one difficult triple jump after another—*seven* in all! Tara skated her entire routine without a single mistake. That night in Nashville, Tara Lipinski made skating history: She became the youngest person ever to win the U.S. Women's Figure Skating Championships!

Two weeks later, Tara and Michelle had a rematch at an international skating championship in Canada. Michelle's fans were hoping that she would bounce back after her one off night in Nashville. But again she fell. And again Tara took the gold medal.

So much had changed for these young skaters in just two weeks! Michelle had been Tara's older idol. Now the two girls were true rivals! Stories comparing Tara and Michelle started to appear in newspapers and magazines across the country. And pressure was building toward the third and most important competition of the season: the World Figure Skating Championships in Lausanne, Switzerland. Could Michelle hold on to her title as the best skater in the world? Or would Tara become the new world champion—the youngest woman ever to win that title?

On the road to Olympic gold, the World Figure Skating Championships are the most important stop. The last three women to win Olympic gold—Katarina Witt, Kristi Yamaguchi, and Oksana Baiul—all won the world championship in the year before the Olympics. That was one of the reasons both Tara and Michelle tried so hard to win that competition. They both hoped to top off their skating careers with an Olympic gold medal.

As you'll find out later in this book, both Tara and Michelle skated well at the World Figure Skating Championships. Of course, there could be only one first-place winner. But the judging was close enough that both girls must have gained more confidence in their skating abilities. And after the World Championships, both Tara and Michelle set their sights on winning a medal at the 1998 Olympics in Japan.

But for two girls who share a dream and have so many things in common, Tara and Michelle have very different personalities and styles. One way to understand their differences is to compare the "good luck" necklaces Tara and Michelle wore at the World Championships.

Beneath her red-and-gold skating costume, Michelle wore a gold charm tied to a piece of silk cord. The charm, showing a Chinese dragon, was a gift from Michelle's grandmother. Michelle

wears the necklace constantly, both for g
and as a reminder of her Chinese heritage

Michelle's parents had lived in Hong Kong before moving to California. When Michelle was born on July 7, 1980, in Torrance, California, her parents gave her a Chinese middle name— Michelle Wing San Kwan. They told her that, by the Chinese calendar, she was born in the Year of the Monkey. And they taught her to understand and speak the Cantonese dialect that they had used in Hong Kong.

Michelle was the youngest of three children in a very busy household. Mr. and Mrs. Kwan divided their attention between their jobs and their children, teaching them traditional Chinese values like hard work, discipline, and respect.

Tara Lipinski, on the other hand, had her parents' undivided attention while she was growing up. She was an only child, with light brown ringlets, bangs, and a huge smile. When Tara decided to become a figure skater, her parents turned their lives upside down in order to help her. Tara and her mother moved to an apartment in Delaware to be near Tara's first coach. Then they moved to an apartment in Michigan when Tara switched to a different coach. The whole time, Tara's father stayed behind in Texas, working to pay the skating bills. The family talked on the phone every night and visited each other once a month.

At the World Championships, beneath the frills of her white skating outfit, Tara wore a gold necklace with the words *Short but Good* dangling from the chain. The necklace summed up both Tara's petite size and her tremendous talents. While Michelle was known for her artistry on the ice, Tara was known for her athletic jumps. Where Michelle was famous for the exotic character roles she played in her programs, Tara was famous for her youthful energy.

Later in this book, you'll find out how these two very different girls are chasing the same dream of Olympic gold. But first, you'll read their separate stories of growing up, from each girl's very first time on skates to the sacrifices they made for their sport, right up to the triumphs and tragedies of the 1997 U.S. Figure Skating Championships and beyond.

In this unforgettable time in Michelle's and Tara's lives, their separate stories have become one—the story of two young ladies, each trying her hardest to be the best figure skater in the world, and each trying to be first on the road to Olympic gold.

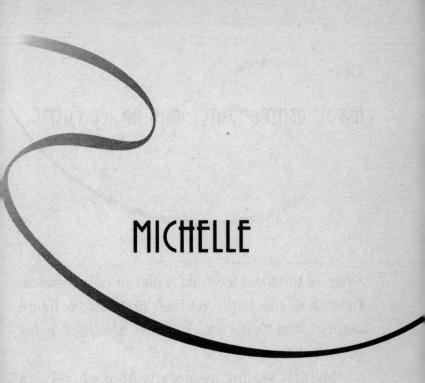

MICHELLE

ONE

NERDS, RENTAL SKATES, AND AN ICE CASTLE

A trip to the local ice rink. A pair of rental skates. That's how most kids get their first taste of figure skating. And that's exactly how it all began for Michelle Kwan.

"My first skating memory is from when I was six," Michelle says. "I was wearing rental skates and eating Nerds candy."

Even though she can't remember that far back, Michelle was actually five the first time she put on a pair of skates. Her parents had taken her to an ice rink to watch her ten-year-old brother, Ron, practice ice hockey.

At first, Michelle sat patiently with her seven-year-old sister, Karen, watching Ron zip up and down the rink. But soon the sisters wanted a turn on the ice, too.

When Ron's practice was over, Michelle and Karen begged their parents to rent them skates. Danny and Estella Kwan saw how excited their daughters were. And they couldn't resist their smiles. So they paid the rental fee and helped the girls lace up.

Michelle and Karen started out like most beginning skaters. They held on to the rail. Then, with their ankles wobbling, they carefully slid their blades along the ice. They fell down and got up again, sometimes hurting, sometimes laughing.

It didn't take long for both girls to discover that they loved skating. Even on the bright sunny days that California is famous for, the Kwan sisters wanted to be inside the ice rink near their home in Torrance.

Soon Michelle and Karen were ready for lessons. But even at the beginner level, skating lessons were expensive. Could the Kwans afford lessons for both girls?

Estella and Danny Kwan were not rich. But they were very hard workers. Estella had grown up in Hong Kong. Danny had grown up in Canton, China. When they emigrated to California in the early 1970s, they both worked at the Golden Pheasant, a restaurant owned by Danny's father. Danny Kwan also worked full-time as a systems analyst for Pacific Bell, the local telephone company.

Of course, the Kwans knew that skating lessons would be costly. But seeing their daughters so happy was worth the price. In the Kwan family, the rules were simple and traditional. *Work hard. Be disciplined. Respect other people. And do what makes you happy.*

Sure enough, Michelle and Karen worked hard in their lessons. They were fast learners. Michelle entered her first competition when she was six—and won!

When Michelle was seven, a television event changed her life. It was the 1988 Winter Olympics in Calgary, Alberta, in Canada. She remembers the thrill she felt on the day that an American skater named Brian Boitano won a gold medal in figure skating. The fans went wild. They waved American flags. That's when Michelle decided that someday she would win a gold medal, too.

Remember, Michelle was only seven when she started thinking about Olympic medals. She had no idea how much training it would take to qualify for the Olympics. She could never have dreamed how much she would have to sacrifice. In her mind, it was simple: She'd skate a lot. She'd work hard. And pretty soon, she'd have an Olympic gold medal to wear around her neck.

Dreaming about the Olympics, Michelle would glide along the ice in a graceful spiral, one leg stretched in the air behind her. She also began to master various jumps. The easiest were the toe loops, where a skater takes off and lands on the same back outside edge of her skates. Then there was the Salchow, where a skater takes off from the inside edge of one foot and lands on the outside edge of the other foot. Lutzes were harder. And so were axels—the only jump where a skater takes off from a forward position.

Sometimes all of these skating terms must have sounded as foreign to Michelle and Karen as the Chinese language that their parents had taught them. But the girls quickly picked up the terms and learned the steps. The sisters rarely fought. And if they were ever jealous of each other, they never showed it. They had been raised to respect each other. And that's exactly what they did.

By 1990, Michelle and Karen were ready to move up to the next skating level. Their parents hired one of the top coaches in the world, Frank Carroll, to work with the girls. Frank Carroll was a polite, quiet man in his fifties, a coach so trustworthy that a reporter called him the "Mr. Rogers of figure skating."

Frank Carroll worked with the Kwan sisters one weekend and immediately spotted their potential. A year later, he asked them to make a big change in their lives. He wanted them to move to the International Ice Castle Training Center in Lake Arrowhead, California.

For serious skaters, Ice Castle is a dream come true. The fourteen-acre training center is tucked among pine trees, high in the San Bernardino Mountains. Skaters often live there year-round, in dormitories or clapboard cottages scattered through the woods. Some Ice Castle skaters attend the local Rim of the World High School. Others spend so much time skating in competitions that they have to be taught by private tutors.

Were Michelle and Karen ready for Ice Castle? Michelle was only eleven years old. Karen was thirteen. Did they love skating enough to leave their home and their school in Torrance?

The Kwans decided to let their girls move to Lake Arrowhead. After all, it wasn't as if they were moving to the other side of the country. Ice Castle was just a two-hour drive from Torrance. At first, Danny Kwan commuted almost daily from Torrance to Lake Arrowhead, making the two-hour drive after a long day at work. Ronnie Kwan stayed in Torrance, where he played high school football and surfed. Eventually, Estella Kwan moved to Ice Castle, so there would always be at least one parent with the girls.

Michelle and Karen began a rigorous training

schedule at Ice Castle. But they weren't alone. The sisters were now part of a group of boys and girls who loved skating as much as they did. They ate their meals together, trained together, and relaxed in the main lodge. They practiced in a beautiful indoor rink, with full-length mirrors and picture windows that looked out on pine trees and wooded paths. Michelle once described life at the Ice Castle as one big slumber party, *except* for the early-morning practices!

A very generous couple, Carol and Walter Probst, owned Ice Castle. They were known to their skaters simply as Mr. and Mrs. P. Mrs. P. had performed with the Ice Follies. She was especially fond of the Kwan sisters. She gave Michelle and Karen free time on the big ice rink and helped pay for their food and lodging.

At first, Michelle just tagged along when her older sister traveled to competitions. But she was a very determined skater. Mr. Kwan remembers taking both girls to the 1991 U.S. Figure Skating Championships in Minneapolis, Minnesota. In the skating world, this event is known as the Nationals.

While Karen had qualified to compete in the Nationals that year, Michelle was forced to practice in a small outdoor rink. "I'm never doing this again," Michelle said earnestly. "I'm not coming just to watch."

True to her word, Michelle qualified to compete on the junior level in the 1992 Nationals in Orlando, Florida. She put herself under a lot of pressure. In fact, she worked so hard to prepare for the event that her parents grew concerned. Danny Kwan urged Michelle not to take the competition so seriously. "It's nothing," he told her repeatedly.

Michelle heard her father's message. She knew he was right. Even so, she couldn't relax. Danny Kwan says he woke up one night and heard Michelle talking in her sleep. She was saying "It's nothing, it's nothing" over and over again. Mr. Kwan was very upset. He hated to see his daughter under so much stress at such an early age.

When it finally came time for Michelle to skate in the Nationals, she placed ninth in the competition. She was so disappointed that she started to cry. That's when Mr. Kwan decided that Michelle needed to change her attitude about skating.

"You are my daughter," Mr. Kwan told Michelle. "Skating has cost a lot of time and money and worry to your parents. But when I see you get too stressed out like this, I think it's time to quit." Mr. Kwan told Michelle that if she wasn't happy skating, it was pointless to compete.

Michelle thought about her father's advice. Was it *really* time to quit? Maybe it was just time to take all of those competitions a little less seriously and make skating a little more fun. And that's exactly what Michelle did—as least for a while. Soon she was pleading with her coach to let her compete at the senior level. Michelle was convinced she could pass the highest level, or "gold," test that all junior skaters must take in order to become senior skaters.

But Coach Carroll refused to let Michelle take the gold test. He said she just wasn't old enough. After all, she wasn't even twelve yet!

Michelle was young, but she was also determined. She wanted to challenge herself by competing against the older skaters. But what could she do? She had been taught to respect her elders. She had always followed her coach's wishes. But for once, Michelle thought, it was time to break the rules.

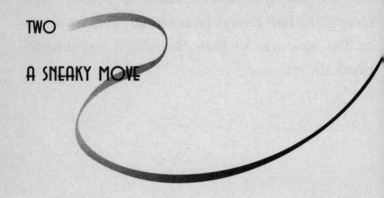

TWO

A SNEAKY MOVE

Michelle came up with a plan. She waited until a weekend in May 1992 when Coach Carroll was out of town. Then she asked her father if she could take the test to compete as a senior.

She told her father she could do all of the jumps required to pass the test. She told him she was ready to compete against the best skaters in the world. But there was one thing she didn't tell her father. She didn't tell him that Coach Carroll had refused to let her take the gold test.

Mr. Kwan simply assumed that Michelle had her coach's permission. It never occurred to him that Michelle would do something behind her coach's back. So of course Mr. Kwan said it was okay for Michelle to take the test.

Michelle didn't feel guilty as she glided onto the ice. "I didn't feel anything," she remembers. "I just did it."

The judges studied Michelle's every move to see if the tiny eleven-year-old had what it took to compete as a senior skater. Here's what Michelle had to do to pass the test:

Jumps

1) At least four different double or triple jumps, including a double Lutz.

2) Two jump combinations consisting of two double jumps or a double and triple jump of the skater's choice.

Spins

1) At least four spins.

2) One of those four spins must be a flying spin. One must be a spin combination consisting of at least two positions and at least one change of foot.

Steps

1) One serpentine step sequence of advanced difficulty.

2) Connecting moves and steps should be demonstrated throughout the program.

3) All of the above should be of championship caliber, performed in good form, and skated with style, rhythm, grace, and sureness.

Michelle completed every requirement. But passing the test turned out to be the easy part. Telling Coach Carroll what she'd done was the hard part!

"I was flabbergasted that this eleven-year-old would go ahead without my blessing," Frank Carroll recalled. "And she wasn't exactly apologetic. She said she wanted to challenge herself against the best. What was I going to do, stand her in the corner for a month?"

Coach Carroll had some stern words for Michelle. He told her there was much more to competing as a senior skater than being able to land double and triple jump combinations. Senior skaters were grown women—elegant, artistic, and dramatic. Yet here she was—Michelle Kwan, a pixieish skater with a cute little ponytail, weighing barely seventy pounds. How could she *ever* get the judges to take her seriously?

"I scared her, and she deserved to be scared, because she was naughty to do what she did," Carroll said. But there was no turning back now.

"Believe me, little girl," Coach Carroll told Michelle, "we have our work cut out for us."

And work they did. Michelle trained on the ice three hours a day, seven days a week. She practiced her triple jumps and her double axels. She had to put together a short program and a long program for competitions. In the short program, Michelle had to complete eight required moves within two minutes and forty seconds. In the long program, also called the free skate or freestyle, Michelle was required to have a routine that lasted four minutes. She'd be judged on her style, choice of music, and technical ability.

To build up her strength, Michelle worked out in the gym and lifted weights. To add gracefulness to her skating, she also worked with a ballet instructor. She spent so much time training that a normal school schedule was out of the question. Michelle began to work with a private tutor two and a half hours a day, five days a week.

Occasionally, Michelle found the time for some typical twelve-year-old hobbies. She collected baseball caps, stationery, bottle caps, and troll dolls in all shapes and sizes. She went to the movies and went bowling or shopping with friends. She loved to play her favorite game— Monopoly. But if someone said "Let's go skiing" or "Let's go sledding," Michelle often had to say no. She was a skater above all else, and she had to be careful not to hurt herself in any other sports.

Michelle's discipline and sacrifices began to pay off in competitions. In fact, she did better as a senior skater than she had as a junior! Michelle won four major events, including the 1993 U.S. Olympic Festival. She amazed the crowd when she landed six triple jumps during her program. And the crowd amazed *her!* There were 25,691 people in the stands—the largest crowd in skating history.

Michelle was the youngest skater ever to win the Olympic Festival. She then set her sights on the 1994 U.S. Figure Skating Championships. Michelle would be competing against the best American female skaters for a spot on the U.S. Olympic team. Did Michelle stand a chance against the elegant Nancy Kerrigan, or the athletic Tonya Harding, or the sophisticated Nicole Bobek?

The 1994 Nationals turned out to be one of the most memorable events in figure skating history. But the memories were bad ones, not good ones. Just two days before the ladies' event, Michelle was practicing alongside Nancy Kerrigan in Cobo Hall in downtown Detroit. Nancy Kerrigan was one of the most admired skaters in the world. She had grace, beauty, and charm, and she wore elegant designer costumes. Next to Nancy, Michelle looked like a little girl.

Michelle will never forget what happened after she and Nancy finished practicing. "People were going: 'Nancy, Nancy, I want your auto-graph.' So I let her go ahead of me. And just as she walked through the curtain, I heard a big scream."

Someone had attacked Nancy Kerrigan! The elegant skater was on the floor, in her white lace practice dress, sobbing in pain. An unknown man had suddenly appeared and clubbed Nancy on the right knee. Then he had fled. In all the confu-sion, Michelle was pushed through the curtain. She didn't know what to do. Things like this were not supposed to happen in the quiet, respectable world of figure skating.

Who had wanted to hurt Nancy Kerrigan? And why? Was it a crazed fan? Or was someone trying to keep Nancy from competing? It would be weeks before the horrible truth came out. But with the competition just two days away, one thing was clear: Nancy Kerrigan, the popular favorite, had suffered a serious injury. She would not be taking part in the ladies' event.

Nancy's absence left the door wide open for her main rival, Tonya Harding. Tonya poured all of her energy into her jumps and won the championship. Then, when Nicole Bobek did not skate well, Michelle ended up in second place! It was an amazing accomplishment for a thirteen-year-old girl.

In any other year, Michelle's second-place finish would have guaranteed her a spot on the U.S. Olympic team. In any other year, she would have become the youngest American athlete in Olympic history. But the attack on Nancy Kerrigan had changed everything.

THREE

THE '94 OLYMPICS—ALMOST

There were two spots open on the Olympic team. By winning the Nationals in Detroit, Tonya had earned one of those spots. And technically, by winning second place, Michelle Kwan had earned the other spot.

But skating officials couldn't just ignore Nancy Kerrigan. Was it Nancy's fault that she hadn't been able to compete in the Nationals? Certainly not. Would Michelle have finished in second place if Nancy had competed? It was hard to say.

Nancy was recovering from her injury. And

the whole country was cheering for her. So the United States Figure Skating Association decided to give the second spot on the Olympic team to Nancy Kerrigan. Michelle became an alternate.

Michelle could have lost her temper. She could have whined like a spoiled teenager. But that had never been her style. Even when reporters asked her if she felt angry, she was her usual gracious, polite self.

"It's a bummer for me," she said. "But I was kind of hoping Nancy would be able to go. She deserves it."

As the '94 Winter Olympics in Lillehammer, Norway, drew closer, the Nancy Kerrigan story took an amazing twist. Police arrested Tonya Harding's ex-husband, Jeff Gillooly, and her bodyguard. The two men were charged with planning and carrying out the attack on Nancy! Had Tonya known about their plans? Had she been in on their scheme? No one knew for sure.

What a complicated mess! Now skating officials had to decide whether they should let Tonya keep her spot on the Olympic team. At first, she claimed to know nothing about the attack. Many people found that hard to believe. But since Tonya hadn't been found guilty of any crime, officials had to let her go to Norway.

Even as the skating world turned against Tonya Harding, Michelle refused to say anything negative about her. When asked about Tonya, Michelle would respond with a simple compliment. She'd tell reporters that Tonya did a great triple axel. And she would leave it at that.

It was a tough time for Michelle's coach and parents. Lawyers started calling the Kwans, offering to sue people if Michelle didn't make the Olympic team. The Kwans didn't like these calls, and they didn't like the publicity. They hired an agent for Michelle, a man named Shep Goldberg, to help them deal with the press.

Mr. and Mrs. Kwan and Coach Carroll tried their best to stay out of the Kerrigan-Harding fight. "We don't pay attention to it," Danny Kwan told a reporter. "Michelle just wants to skate. That's the bottom line."

As the Kerrigan-Harding rivalry continued to

make front-page news, Michelle quietly packed her bags and flew to Norway for the 1994 Olympics. But she was only there in case Nancy or Tonya was unable to skate. The U.S. Olympic Committee didn't let her stay with all the other athletes in the Olympic Village. Instead, they arranged for Michelle and her parents to stay in a hotel in Oslo, far removed from the excitement of the Olympic Village.

But Michelle couldn't just relax in her hotel room, reading books or watching TV. She had to be prepared to skate on short notice, so she had to stay in top shape. Arrangements were made for her to practice in a nearby ice rink.

"It was freezing cold and lonely," Michelle remembers. "I was all by myself, skating in this big rink." Even so, Michelle worked hard, perfecting the seven triple jumps in her program.

As it turned out, Michelle never had the chance to perform that program before an Olympic audience. Both Nancy and Tonya skated, but with mixed results.

Tonya was in tenth place going into the long

program. She didn't seem very well prepared for the Olympics. She'd left her plastic skate guards at home in Oregon. And when it came time for her long program, she had problems with her laces, making her late on the ice. After missing her first triple Lutz, Tonya started to cry. She skated over to the judges and begged for a second chance.

It was an embarrassing scene for the entire American team. Eventually, Tonya returned with a longer lace and finished in eighth place.

Nancy, on the other hand, skated what she thought was the best performance of her life in the long program. She was graceful, and she landed smoothly on all five of her triple jumps. Nancy must have been sure she'd won as she skated over to the "Kiss and Cry" area to await her scores.

But Nancy lost—by just one-tenth of a point—to the Ukrainian skater Oksana Baiul. Nancy came home with the silver medal, never to compete in the Olympics again. When Tonya returned home, she was fined for not helping in the official investigation of the Kerrigan attack. And she was kicked out of the United States Figure Skating Association.

Unlike Tonya and Nancy, Michelle Kwan knew she'd get another chance at the Olympics. What she had been through "didn't feel like an Olympic experience," Michelle said. "I never really got to see the ice rink. I never got to see the Olympic Village." She wanted the real thing. The next opportunity was four years away, in Nagano, Japan. But it was never too early to dream.

Back home in her cottage at Ice Castle, Michelle put a big sticker over her dresser that said NAGANO 1998! Every night she'd see that sticker before falling asleep after a long day of training. "In my dreams," she said, "I'm crying because I'm happy and I have the gold medal. Then I wake up and think, 'Oh darn.'"

Of course, there were days when Michelle woke up and just didn't feel like training, Olympics or not. When a reporter from *Girl* magazine asked her if she always liked to practice, she gave an honest answer:

"Once in a while I wake up and I'm like, 'UGHHH. I don't want to skate.' I might feel like that, but I know I want to keep myself in good shape. If I feel tired, I just take it easy on the ice and don't force myself to do something that I'm too tired to do, because you can get hurt easily in skating. If you were tired on the morning of the Olympics, you couldn't say, 'Oh, I don't want to skate.' I just take each day as it comes."

And just how did she spend a typical day? The reporter from *Girl* magazine was exhausted just listening to Michelle describe her schedule:

"I wake up at around 8:30 and eat breakfast. I start skating at 10:15 for forty-five minutes. Then I go back down and do my homework. After this, I go back up to the rink and skate for another forty-five minutes. Then I go back to the lodge and do more homework. My tutor comes from 3:30 to 5:30. At 5:30, I go and eat dinner and then I go back up to the rink at 6:30 and skate. I also work out in the gym or do ballet at night."

Michelle took her schoolwork very seriously, even though she was never in a typical classroom. When she left for competitions, she stayed in touch with her tutor by using a laptop computer. She received her homework from her tutor via E-mail. And she sent it back the same way.

To make up for the time she spent skating and competing, Michelle had to study year-round. Even during Christmas vacation. Even during the summer! But there was at least one good thing about mixing skating and studying: In 1995, when her schedule was packed with world history, algebra, English, French, and calligraphy, Michelle was allowed to skip one required subject—physical education. No one had to worry about Michelle Kwan *not* getting enough exercise!

But there were other concerns as Michelle prepared for the 1995 Nationals in Providence, Rhode Island. In less than two years, she had grown seven inches and gained nineteen pounds.

She was now five feet two and weighed ninety-six pounds. She wasn't overweight—not by a long shot! But her coach was concerned that her natural growth spurt might easily throw off her balance on her triple jumps.

Michelle was the early favorite in the Nationals. But she ran into some problems in her short program. A mistake on her double jump combination–triple Lutz–double toe loop–left her in third place, behind a twenty-three year-old college graduate, Tonia Kwiatkowski, and the often-injured and unpredictable Nicole Bobek.

On the night of the long program, Michelle was the last to skate. She never liked that position, because of the long wait. When she finally took her turn on the ice, she skated well—right up until her second triple Lutz. She didn't get the speed or height she needed and fell right on her hip. A disappointed Michelle finished in second place, behind Nicole Bobek.

Michelle and Coach Carroll returned to Lake Arrowhead, determined to make a better showing at the World Championships in Birmingham,

England. They changed the order of her jumps in the short program, putting the more difficult combinations first. When Michelle returned to the ice in England, she performed her new short program perfectly. But the judges gave higher scores to the older skaters.

"I skated like it's a sport, went for everything I've got, and just gave it my best shot," Michelle said at a press conference. "You might be the best in your heart, but not in other people's sight."

The night of the long program competition, Michelle again gave it her best shot. She landed five triples. Perfectly. She landed the triple Lutz that had caused her nasty fall in Providence. No problem. Ponytail flying, smiling widely, she even threw in an extra double toe loop.

Michelle's eyes were filled with happy tears by the time she landed her last triple. She received the only standing ovation of the evening. Even so, she finished in fourth place. Why hadn't the judges given her higher scores?

In Coach Carroll's opinion, the judges thought Michelle looked too young. "I'd put her in a very simple dress because I wanted her to look fresh and young, and the judges didn't buy it," Coach Carroll told a reporter. "They didn't want a fresh young girl. They wanted the ladies' champion of the world. They wanted sophistication and emotion and drama."

Back in Lake Arrowhead, Coach Carroll realized it was time for a new strategy. He wanted to give Michelle a "makeover" so she'd look more mature for the judges. He wanted her to wear mascara, lipstick, a new hairdo—the works! But Michelle was not easily convinced. And neither, it turned out, were her parents.

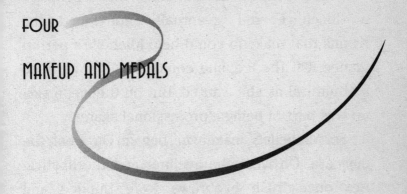

FOUR

MAKEUP AND MEDALS

Many fourteen year-old girls would love it if an adult told them they *had* to wear makeup. Not Michelle. "I was afraid to jump with mascara on," she giggled. "I didn't think I'd be able to see."

That wasn't her only concern. Her parents thought it was inappropriate for young teenage girls to try and look like older women.

"Her Chinese background is, you don't wear makeup at that age," Coach Carroll later explained to a reporter. "I had to say: 'If you're appearing in the ballet, you have to look the part. There's nothing extraordinary about wearing makeup. It's part of the shtick. We're not taking school exams, we're performing in front of thousands of people.'"

Coach Carroll eventually convinced the Kwans that makeup could help Michelle's performance. Off the ice, she could still look as fresh and natural as she wanted. But on the ice, makeup was part of being a professional skater.

So Michelle's makeover began. On went the mascara. On went the eyeliner and the lipstick. Her once-girlish eyebrows were thinned and shaped. Away went the ponytail, replaced by a bun that was braided, wrapped, and secured tightly to her head.

Those were the changes people could see. But more important were the changes Michelle must have felt inside. Now that she was fifteen years old, Michelle said she had a better idea of the dramatic skills she needed to develop.

"When I was fourteen," she explained, "I didn't know much of anything. I never really developed my skating. I just jumped and jumped and jumped some more. It wasn't really artistic. I kind of smiled every once in a while and laughed it off.

But you want to feel what's inside and be able to portray it and express it to the audience."

To complete Michelle's transformation, Coach Carroll assigned her a role to play. In her long program, she would perform as the biblical character Salome. It was a very daring decision.

In the Bible, Salome is the stepdaughter of Herod, the governor of Galilee. At a birthday party for Herod, Salome performs the dance of the seven veils. Herod is so moved by Salome's beautiful dancing that he offers to grant her any wish. Salome wishes for the head of St. John the Baptist. Herod has John the Baptist beheaded. And he sends Salome the head on a platter!

Of course, Michelle couldn't end her skating performance carrying a head on a platter. That part was left out. But everything else was true to Salome's character, from the exotic music to her jeweled costume.

Michelle first appeared as Salome in the fall of 1995, at a competition called Skate America. She looked so different in her makeup and grown-up costume that at first no one recognized her.

People stared. Then they started asking, "Who's that girl with Frank Carroll?"

Coach Carroll was overjoyed. Even before Michelle skated, he knew the judges would treat her differently. "I knew we had 'em," Carroll said.

He was right. Michelle won first place at Skate America. And first place at Skate Canada. Then first place again at both the Nations Cup and the U.S. Postal Service Challenge.

Michelle was on a roll. But would her luck hold out until the 1996 U.S. Figure Skating Championships? After two years of placing second at the Nationals, Michelle was ready to go for the gold.

The entire Kwan family must have been especially excited about that year's Nationals. And it wasn't just because Michelle had her best chance ever to win. The Kwans were also happy because the championship was being held in their home state of California. On top of that, Karen Kwan, now seventeen years old, was also having a good year and was expected to do well at the Nationals.

When it was Karen's turn on the ice, no one was disappointed. Michelle's older sister finished in a very respectable fifth place. That meant a lot to Michelle, who had never stopped supporting Karen's skating career.

Even when Michelle came in first place at the Nationals, her thoughts were on Karen. "My happiest moment wasn't when I won the gold," said Michelle. "It was when I saw Karen skate so well."

Michelle was the youngest woman to win the Nationals in thirty-two years. In many ways, she was still just a kid at heart. On the ice, she was the glamorous Salome. But when she left the rink, gold medal in hand, she still carried a teddy bear knapsack. And she still had a little girl's crush on the star of the TV show *Baywatch*. "When I met David Hasselhoff," she told a reporter, "I thought, 'Oh, my god, I'm going to faint.'"

Two months after winning the Nationals, Michelle headed to Edmonton, Alberta. This was no time to think about crushes. No time to think about anyone or anything except skating. It was March 1996, and Michelle was now hoping to become not just the best skater in the country, but the best skater in the world.

Two other skaters from the United States would also be competing at the World Figure Skating Championships. One was Tonia Kwiatkowski, now twenty-four. The other was thirteen-year-old Tara Lipinski. Michelle was probably very pleased to see this young skater making so much progress. But Michelle's toughest competition was expected to come from Lu Chen of China, who had won the previous year's title and was determined to keep it.

Michelle got off to an excellent start in the short program. Not only did she jump well, she also skated with elegance and poise, gliding across the ice in what her coach called a graceful "ooze." Seven of the nine judges gave her marks of 5.9. That was just one-tenth of a point away from a perfect score of 6.

Heading into the long program, Michelle needed to gather her thoughts. Coach Carroll took her to the only quiet place he could find in the Edmonton Coliseum—a small space set aside for the flower girls who picked up bouquets that had been thrown onto the ice.

But it wasn't quiet enough. Michelle and her coach could still hear the loudspeaker as it announced Chen's scores. They included two perfect marks of 6.0 for artistic merit.

It would take every ounce of Michelle's energy to top those scores. Michelle knew it. So did her coach. "I had about two seconds to say something intelligent and meaningful before she had to go out and skate," Carroll remembers. "So I told her those were fabulous marks, but the judges had left room for her to win."

Michelle Kwan looked at her coach. "You're right," she said calmly.

"I knew right then she was going to win," Carroll told a reporter. And Michelle felt it, too. "Nothing could stop me," she said. "If a brick wall had been on the ice, I would have just rammed through it."

In the most memorable performance of her career, Michelle landed the six triple jumps she had rehearsed. She was a picture of grace, from the slightest movement of her hand down to the clean edges of her blades. And in a daring move, Michelle even threw in an extra, unrehearsed triple toe loop at the end of her program, hoping to win an advantage over Lu Chen.

The stands of the Edmonton Coliseum shook with applause. And this time, the judges were just as enthusiastic. Michelle received two 6.0's of her own for artistic merit. The seven other judges awarded her 5.9's—enough to seal her victory over Lu Chen.

At first, Michelle was in shock. "I'm a world champion. I can't believe it," she said. "It has not really gone to my brain yet."

But when she had time to think about it more, she realized that she had earned her title. "I know I'm supposed to be surprised by what I've accomplished," she said later. "But why should I be? Everyone says it happened so fast, but it didn't seem fast to me. I was out there every day, all the time working and skating well."

As Michelle set off on a fifty-stop tour, her parents must have been very relieved. Top-name skaters like Michelle could earn up to $12,000 for every show they performed on tour. The money from Michelle's appearances gave a huge boost to the family finances. The Kwans had been spending about $60,000 a year on Michelle and Karen's training. They had even sold their first big home to help pay for the cost of their daughters' careers. Now Michelle was on her way to becoming a millionaire!

On tour, Michelle always traveled with her mother or father. Often both parents went along. Danny and Estella Kwan still kept a watchful eye on their daughter. They did not want her success to go to her head. "Don't start thinking you're special," Mr. Kwan often told Michelle. "The trouble begins when you start building a wall around you."

Once, when Michelle was on tour, her father saw her hurry onto the bus after a performance, ignoring the fans who had gathered to see her.

That prompted one of Mr. Kwan's fatherly lectures. Families often paid hundreds of dollars to come to a show, he told Michelle. "Never ignore your fans," Mr. Kwan said sternly. "All the things you have come from them. Learn to give back."

Michelle learned her lesson. She immediately got off the bus and signed autographs for her eager fans, drawing a little heart before her name. Never again would she skip out a back door.

Michelle thought of other ways to give back to the community. After performances, fans often showered her with flowers or stuffed animals. She always made sure those gifts ended up in the hands of sick or needy children.

Back home after touring, Michelle continued to receive hundreds of fan letters each week. She took the time to answer each letter with a note and an autographed picture. She often signed those photos, stacks at a time, while her mother stuffed them into envelopes and her father sealed them. "I know how much people appreciate it," Michelle once told a Boston newspaper reporter. "I mean, someone takes the time to write a long letter to you, you can take a little time to sign your name."

As Michelle prepared for a new season, she

was on top of her sport and on top of the world. She seemed unbeatable. "I don't feel like she's been challenged a lot," Coach Carroll told a newspaper reporter just before the 1997 Nationals in Nashville. "But somewhere along the line there's a little girl coming up, and she's going to be good and give her a run for her money. That's healthy. That's life. That's sport. I don't see that right now. But it will come. It always does."

That challenge came a lot sooner than Coach Carroll had predicted. Just two days after he uttered those words, a four-foot eight-inch skater thrilled the crowd at the Nationals. And that tiny girl, of course, was Tara Lipinski.

TARA

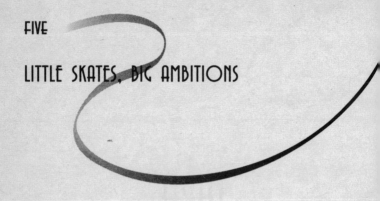

FIVE

LITTLE SKATES, BIG AMBITIONS

Tara Lipinski had been competing on the senior level for only a year when she burst onto the scene at the '97 Nationals. But she had already captured many hearts with her big smile. And many people had already heard the story of her devoted parents who had sacrificed so much to help Tara skate.

Tara was born on June 10, 1982, in Philadelphia. Her mother, Pat, was a former secretary and her father, Jack, was an executive. Tara meant the world to them. She was their only child, and they would do anything to make her happy.

By the age of three, when some kids can barely hop on one foot, Tara was zipping along on roller skates. But she wasn't satisfied just skating around her driveway. Her parents began taking her to roller-skating lessons at a rink near their home in Sewell, New Jersey.

Even as a preschooler, Tara showed signs of athletic talent and ambition. One of her favorite activities was to play roller hockey with older boys. She also started competing in local roller-skating competitions. At the age of five, Tara won her first regional contest!

Without brothers or sisters to play with, Tara was always on the lookout for fun ways to pass the time. One rainy day, when Tara was six, her mother suggested ice skating. Pat Lipinski took Tara to a local rink. What happened that day changed Tara's life.

Within minutes, Tara was on the ice, skating just as smoothly as if she were on roller skates. And within an hour, Mrs. Lipinski remembers,

Tara had transferred everything she had learned from roller skating to ice skating. She began doing jumps and turns on the ice, immediately falling in love with this newly discovered sport.

Tara didn't put her roller skates away for good. But from that day on, ice skating was her passion. Her parents say they tried to interest her in other activities, like horseback riding and modeling. But all she wanted to do was skate.

The University of Delaware had one of the best skating centers in the country. So Mr. and Mrs. Lipinski started taking their daughter there for lessons.

Tara began her figure-skating lessons the year of the 1988 Winter Olympics. Was she just as inspired by the 1988 Olympics as Michelle Kwan? The way she remembers it, she certainly was. A few days before the '97 Nationals, she told *New York Times* reporter Jere Longman a funny story. She said that she remembers asking her father to build her a pretend victory podium out of boxes after watching the Olympics in 1988. No matter which athlete she was pretending to be, she

Twelve-year-old Michelle performs a spiral at the 1992 Junior Championships.

Twelve-year-old Tara strikes a graceful pose at the 1994 U.S. Olympic Festival.

The scores are in...

...and Tara shares a celebratory hug with her coach.

Michelle (right) and her older sister, Karen, lace up for a practice session.

Michelle perfects a spin at her home rink in Lake Arrowhead, California.

Michelle turns in a gold-medal performance
at the 1996 Figure Skating Championships
in San Jose, California.

Tara waves to the crowd following
her near-flawless short program
at the 1997 World Championships
in Lausanne, Switzerland.

Michelle off the ice…

…but never very far from the ri

Tara wows the crowd during the Champions' Exhibition at the 1997 U.S. National Championships in Nashville, Tennessee.

After one of the closest finishes ever
in a women's World Championship,
Tara and Michelle look forward to future competitions!

always stood on the top box, where the gold medalist stood. It was the gold medal she wanted. Only gold.

Tara's father later questioned that account. "It makes me look bad, the story about the boxes," Mr. Lipinski said. "It was like I was already at that age pushing her to be champion." In his version of the story, Tara wasn't five and a half years old. She was fourteen, watching the 1996 Summer Olympic games in Atlanta. And every time a national anthem would play, Tara would stand not on a box but a Tupperware bowl. So much for family folklore!

The Lipinskis say they never pushed little Tara to compete. It was clear to them from the start that Tara loved skating more than anything in the world. And, like most parents, all they wanted was to make their child happy.

In 1991, Mr. Lipinski received word that he'd been assigned to Houston, to serve as vice president of an oil company called Coastal Corporation. That meant Tara had to say goodbye to her friends, her school, and her skating coach in

Delaware. She was nine years old when she moved to Texas.

The Lipinskis bought a home in a suburb called Sugar Land, not far from Houston. Texas was a big, sprawling state. But it wasn't exactly overflowing with opportunities for young figure skaters.

The closest place for Tara to skate was a rink in the Galleria shopping mall in Houston. The rink was crowded and very distracting for a focused skater like Tara. In order to have some private time on the ice, Tara had to get up at three in the morning. She skated in the early hours before school.

Tara's new coach was a woman named Megan Faulkner. Coach Faulkner admired Tara's determination. She knew it was hard for Tara to skate in a public shopping mall. But there was little she could do to improve the skating conditions for her talented pupil.

The shoppers weren't the only distraction. Once, during the December holiday season, the mall put a huge Christmas tree right in the middle of the rink! Tara tried not to complain. But who wanted to worry about running into a Christmas tree when you were trying to do a double axel?

A less dedicated skater might have quit. But somehow Tara found the energy and discipline to keep up with her lessons. By the time she was eleven, though, her parents were convinced that Tara deserved better. Pat and Jack Lipinski knew that, for Tara's sake, they had to make a major change in their lives.

SIX

A FAMILY DIVIDED

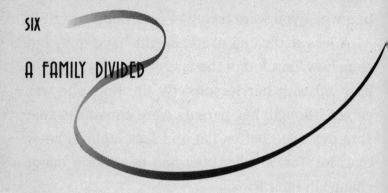

The Lipinskis had a problem. They had decided that Tara needed to return to her old rink at the University of Delaware. But Mr. Lipinski couldn't give up his job and move back East. He needed the income from his work in Houston to help pay for Tara's lessons.

What could they do? One possibility was to have Tara live with a host family, close to the Delaware rink. Living with a host family was a common practice for young athletes, especially those in training for the Olympics. But for Pat and Jack Lipinski, the idea of sending Tara to live with another family was out of the question. Tara was their only child. There *had* to be a better solution.

The plan they finally came up with was not ideal. But under the circumstances, it was the best they could do. Jack Lipinski would stay in Houston to continue providing the family with income. Tara and her mother would move to an apartment near Tara's old rink in Delaware. Tara would rejoin the Delaware Figure Skating Club, where they hoped she would flourish under extremely intensive professional training.

The move must have been extremely difficult. And living twelve hundred miles apart couldn't have been fun. Mr. Lipinski called his wife and daughter every night on the phone and visited at least once a month. But there was no getting around it. Splitting apart the family was a huge sacrifice for all three of the Lipinskis. If Tara hadn't found so much happiness in her skating, all the lonely nights probably would not have been worth it. Not long after the move, Mr. Lipinski told *Primetime Live,* "I miss out on seeing

Tara grow up a lot and it's difficult. We call, we talk. But it's really hard."

And Tara agreed. "He really misses us. He's all alone in that house. It's sad."

Being separated from her father was only one of the big changes in Tara's lifestyle. She also stopped going to a normal school. She needed to spend her mornings on the ice, so her parents paid for a private tutor to work with her in the afternoon.

Tara worked hard under the guidance of her coach, Jeff DiGregorio. She learned to launch herself into the air like a spinning top. What she lacked in height she made up for in speed. And soon, her intensive training started to pay off. At the age of eleven, Tara became the national novice silver medalist. Then, skating at the junior level during the summer of her twelfth birthday, Tara won a gold medal at the U.S. Olympic Festival.

Tara was now the youngest gold medalist in the history of the U.S. Olympic Festival—even younger than Michelle Kwan, who had won that same competition on the senior level just a year earlier.

For the first time, reporters began to take real notice of Tara. She was so tiny. So cute. A fun, bubbly chatterbox. And to think her parents willingly lived apart, just to help Tara's skating career! It was quite a story.

In October 1994, *The New York Times* printed a long profile about Tara Lipinski and her family. The same day the article appeared in the paper, the phone started ringing off the hook at the University of Delaware ice rink. Now the television networks wanted to talk to the Lipinskis! It seemed everyone was interested in this story of a family divided.

Tara made her first television appearance on ABC's *Good Morning America*. Then another ABC show, *Primetime Live,* began talking to the Lipinskis. They wanted to start working on a lengthy story about Tara that would be shown on television the following March.

Christine Brennan, a reporter for the *Washington Post*, came up with a name for all this sudden interest in Tara. In a book she wrote about figure skating, *Inside Edge: A Revealing Journey into the Secret World of Figure Skating*, she called it "Tara-mania!"

Three different agents contacted the Lipinskis. They all wanted Tara as a client. One of those agents, Mike Burg, paid Tara $5,000 to skate in a televised event called *Ice Wars*. That seemed like a lot of money. But it was nothing compared to what the Lipinskis were paying for Tara's lessons. In 1994, they said they spent $58,000 of their own money to pay for Tara's coaches, costumes, skates, ice time, travel expenses, and living expenses in Delaware.

When Tara wasn't at an ice rink, she was often on an airplane. In December 1994, Tara and her mother hopped on a plane to Houston to be with Mr. Lipinski for the holidays. The plan was for the two of them to stay until New Year's Eve. But after spending Christmas Eve and Christmas Day in Texas, Tara grew restless. She felt she should be training in Delaware, so she flew back there for five days, then back to Texas on New Year's Eve.

Mrs. Lipinski reminded Tara that airplane tickets weren't cheap. "I told her, 'Well, if that's what you want to do, fine, that's your Christmas gift. The extra flight, that's the money for your gift.'"

For Tara, the extra time she was able to spend on the ice was indeed the best gift of all. She always told people she was happiest when she was skating. And she had a big event coming up. Tara wanted to do well as a junior skater that February at the Nationals in Providence, Rhode Island.

With all the media attention she had been receiving, Tara was now under extra pressure to do well at the Nationals. Dealing with that pressure wasn't always easy for Mrs. Lipinski. It was especially hard on the day that the TV crew from *Primetime Live* arrived in Delaware to videotape their story about the life of Tara Lipinski.

Christine Brennan described that hectic day in her book *Inside Edge*. First, Mrs. Lipinski was videotaped watching Tara practice. Then Mrs. Lipinski was interviewed for two whole hours. By late in the afternoon, Tara hadn't even had her turn on camera. A weary Mrs. Lipinski snapped at Tara, telling her to stop running around, because she looked like a mess. "How do you think you'll look on TV?" she asked her daughter.

Mrs. Lipinski later apologized. "This is not a normal day," she said. "Honestly, it's never like this."

Even Coach DiGregorio started getting a bit concerned about all the publicity surrounding his young pupil. "I'll just feel horrible if she doesn't skate well or even if she doesn't win, because she's expected to win," he said.

As the grownups in her life worried, Tara did what she does best. She put on a little black velvet dress and black gloves, laced up her skates, and took to the ice in the Providence Civic Center. She was the first to skate in the junior ladies' short program. One after the other, she pulled off a triple loop–double loop combination, a double axel, and a double flip—all without a wobble. Four of her technical marks were above 5.0. That's high for a junior skater. But her artistic marks weren't quite as high, and she came in second behind a fifteen-year-old junior skater named Sydne Vogel.

The junior ladies' long program event was held two days later. This time, Tara performed last on the ice. As she skated to "Samson and Delilah," she successfully managed one jump after another. She even landed a triple jump—a move she had learned only a few days earlier! When Tara left the ice, she thought she had won. Her coach thought so, too. But again her artistic scores were lower. Sydne Vogel took the gold. Tara won the silver.

After a few tears, Tara and her coach went to meet the press. "I would have put Tara first," DiGregorio said proudly. "She was the best in *my* eyes."

A reporter asked Tara if she felt pressured by all the media interest she had received. "I like the cameras," Tara answered. "When I go home, I'll train hard, and next year I'll be back here and have the TV cameras here again."

But Tara didn't have to wait a whole year to be back in front of the television cameras. The very next morning, it was Tara—not Sydne Vogel—who was interviewed on *Good Morning America*. Tara's picture also appeared in *USA Today* and *Sports Illustrated*. The *Primetime Live* story about Tara and her family aired March 1. The segment was eleven minutes long. It didn't seem to matter that Tara had only won the silver at the Nationals. She was still being treated as figure skating's rising star.

Back in Delaware, Coach DiGregorio had big plans for Tara. He was convinced that soon she'd be doing not just triple jumps but *quadruple* jumps in competitions. Later in the year, though, DiGregorio and Mrs. Lipinski had some disagreements. They decided it would be in Tara's best interest to work with a new coach.

To find that new coach, Mrs. Lipinski and Tara crisscrossed the country, checking out one skating center after another. Tara took lessons from some of the best coaches in the world, including Carlo Fassi. Fassi taught at Ice Castle, along with Michelle Kwan's coach, Frank Carroll.

Tara could have chosen Ice Castle, joining

Michelle Kwan and her sister. But in the end, Tara and her mother felt most comfortable with Richard Callaghan, a highly respected coach based in Detroit, Michigan.

As Tara and her mother prepared to move to Detroit, the question of living arrangements came up once again. What about Tara's father? Could he give up his job and move to Detroit? Unfortunately, the answer was no. Mr. Lipinski needed to stay in Houston, working to help finance Tara's dreams of gold.

SEVEN

"SHORT BUT GOOD"

Once in Detroit, Tara and her mother had to adjust to a new apartment, new tutors, and a new rink—not to mention a new coach. At the same time, Richard Callaghan had to get used to his new student and her mother as well.

"You've got to realize in this sport that parents are important," Coach Callaghan once explained. "Probably learning to tolerate all the stress and pressure that goes along with it is an education."

Coach Callaghan and Mrs. Lipinski learned to work out any differences they had concerning

Tara's training. "It's not like we always agree," Callaghan told a reporter. "But I do respect her."

In much the same way, Coach Callaghan respected Tara's amazing determination on the ice. But he didn't always agree with her when she insisted on total perfection. Sometimes, he said, he had to drag her off the ice at the end of a practice session.

"She has in her mind that she has to repeat every jump five times before she leaves the arena to feel comfortable with herself," Callaghan once said. "I don't like that. I've changed that. Tara's a perfectionist. If she doesn't do things right, she gets upset too quickly. I still think she could be easier on herself, but there's no crying."

What did Coach Callaghan say to Tara when she insisted on doing a particular jump ten times over? He had to work out a deal with her. "When it's time to finish and she wants to do more," he once explained, "we discuss why she wants to do more. If she can give me valid reasons, we'll do more. But I still want her to be healthy when she's twenty-four."

As Tara's coach, Richard Callaghan had to make sure Tara didn't hurt herself jumping. He had to make sure her little bones could handle the pressure of triple jump after triple jump after triple jump.

Doctors had reportedly assured Mrs. Lipinski that Tara had a strong muscle and bone structure. But it was also their belief that Tara would probably never grow taller than four feet eleven inches.

Knowing that she'd probably never be a tall skater, Tara learned to make her petite size work to her advantage. As she and Coach Callaghan prepared for the 1996 Nationals in San Jose, California, Tara perfected her own style of jumping. She never seemed to get extremely high off the ice. But somehow she managed to spin her body so tightly that she made even a difficult triple axel look easy.

Tara spent much of her time training with another of Coach Callaghan's students—a young man named Todd Eldredge. Todd was an experienced skater and the men's winner at the 1995

Nationals. But that didn't stop Tara from challenging Todd on the ice. "Anything you can do I can do better," she told him jokingly. If Todd pulled off a perfect triple axel, followed by a double toe loop, she'd insist on doing the same. The friendly bet made both Tara and Todd better skaters.

By the time the '96 Nationals rolled around, Tara and Todd were Coach Callaghan's star skaters. Nicole Bobek had also been part of their training group, but she called it quits with Callaghan just before the Nationals. Changing coaches was nothing new for Nicole. She was now on her ninth coach in fifteen years!

People never quite knew what to expect from Nicole Bobek. And that ended up helping Tara once the competition was under way in San Jose. Just before her long program, Nicole announced that her ankle was too swollen to skate. She was forced to withdraw from the event.

With Nicole out of the picture, there were fewer major competitors for Tara. That was especially important because this was the first year

Tara was competing in the Nationals as a senior skater. As you'll remember, Michelle Kwan easily captured the gold. Tonia Kwiatkowski, the silver medalist, was almost twice Tara's age. Thirteen-year-old Tara must have been very pleased to finish in third place, and happy to have a bronze medal to wear around her neck. But even more important, she was no doubt thrilled that her third-place finish guaranteed her a spot at the 1996 World Championships in Edmonton, Alberta.

Tara had to have been overjoyed. There she was, just thirteen years old, given the chance to compete against the best skaters in the world: Michelle Kwan, Lu Chen of China, Irina Slutskaya of Russia.

When Tara arrived in Edmonton, she tried to forget she was just a seventy-pound thirteen-year-old. She skated well in practice. But the night of her short program, Tara's confidence seemed to melt as she skated onto the ice. At four feet six inches, she looked like a tiny speck on the 17,000 square feet of ice in the Edmonton

Coliseum. And more than 15,000 people from all over the world were watching her every move.

"I was a little nervous going out there," she admitted to a reporter. "It was all a little overwhelming."

Tara had practiced her program until she could practically do it in her sleep. But that night, she must have felt as if she were skating in a nightmare. She wobbled on a triple Lutz. She fell on one of her easiest jumps—a double loop. Then she fell again on her triple flip jump.

What was happening? She looked over at Coach Callaghan, who was standing beside the boards. Help me, her eyes seemed to plead. She found the strength to finish her program, but the damage had been done. She finished twenty-third out of thirty skaters.

Luckily for Tara, twenty-four skaters were allowed to compete in the long program event. She made the cut—although just barely.

Coach Callaghan searched for reasons to explain his pupil's disappointing short program. "She's had a great week here," he told reporters.

"We've probably been here just a little bit too long and then all of a sudden, the pressure of the event maybe got to her a little bit."

Tara was down. But she didn't dwell on her poor performance. She knew she still had another chance in the long program. And she was determined to show the world that she—thirteen-year-old Tara Lipinski—deserved to be competing among the world's best skaters.

In an amazing comeback, Tara landed seven triple jumps in her long program, pulling herself up to a fifteenth-place finish. The crowd jumped to its feet, applauding wildly for that little spinning speck down on the ice.

The standing ovation reassured Tara. It was as if she were five years old again, playing roller hockey with the big boys. She had proved she could play with the big kids and hold her own.

"I was so low, so down, that first day," Tara later told a reporter. "To come back and skate great and get a standing ovation, I knew I could do it. I wanted to show everybody that I deserved to be there."

Tara had shown them, all right. And by the next season, no one would ever wonder again if little Tara Lipinski could make it big.

EIGHT

"LEAPIN' LIPINSKI!"

Like Coach Carroll with Michelle in the summer of 1995, Coach Callaghan faced a challenge in the summer of 1996 with Tara. He wanted to make his pupil look more mature. But he didn't want to bury her in so much makeup that it hid her delightful smile. And he certainly didn't want anything to mask her clear love of skating.

"I want her to look fourteen," Callaghan said, "but a sophisticated fourteen."

Like Michelle, Tara started wearing her hair in a bun instead of a ponytail. She kept her bangs, but she also started wearing a little more lipstick and eye makeup. Most of all, she worked on her skating style. She wanted to be known for something more than her incredible jumps. And like Michelle, she wanted to add grace and elegance to her programs.

Three days a week, Tara worked with ballet instructor Marina Sheffer. Marina helped Tara make her skating look fluid and effortless. That summer, Tara also worked very closely with a well-known choreographer named Sandra Bezic. Sandra had designed Brian Boitano's gold-medal-winning routine for the 1988 Olympics. Now Sandra's challenge would be to help choreograph a long program that would best showcase Tara's talents.

What about the music? Tara's coach began looking for something that would have just the right combination of sophistication and youthful enthusiasm. He found exactly what he wanted in the soundtrack of the 1995 movie *Little Women*. The music brought to mind all the energy and intelligence of the March sisters as they developed into young women. It was perfect for Tara Lipinski—the little woman of figure skating.

The soundtrack from *Little Women* became the music for Tara's short program. For her long program she kept with the same mood, skating to movie soundtracks from *Sense and Sensibility* and *Much Ado About Nothing*.

As Tara geared up for the new season, she had some great days in practice. She also had some days when nothing seemed to go right. But a visit to a children's hospital helped her put her own bad days in perspective.

Tara was visiting City of Hope, a hospital for children with serious illnesses, when she noticed a boy who seemed especially sad. She asked him if he needed anything. He said no—he was just having a bad day. That phrase immediately rang a bell with Tara because she'd said it a thousand times after a bad practice or an unsuccessful jump.

At that moment, Tara realized how very lucky she was. She had her health. And she had the opportunity to do the one thing that brought her the most happiness in the world: skate. Tara decided to try and visit a children's hospital every time she was in a new town for a competition. Learning to give back to the community helped Tara mature off the ice. On the ice, it gave her the strength to get through five-hour training sessions without complaining, even on a bad day.

Tara couldn't wait for the new skating season to get under way. When it did, Tara's passport received as much of a workout as her skates! First stop: Skate Canada, part of the Champions International Skating series.

There, in Kitchener, Ontario, Tara debuted her two new programs. After the short technical program, she was ranked in third place. But she bounced back in the long program to finish in second place behind Irina Slutskaya of Russia. The silver was Tara's first international medal. Her new season was off to a great start!

Tara had one night's sleep in Detroit. Then she was off to Paris, to compete in the Trophée Lalique. This time, Tara found herself competing against Michelle Kwan and Maria Butyrskaya, another dramatic Russian star. Tara captured the bronze, pleased to skate away with her second international medal.

Tara thought she'd be getting a rest after Paris. But when Nicole Bobek suffered another injury, Tara was asked to compete as her replacement in the Nations Cup in Gelsenkirchen, Germany. Once again, Tara performed her programs flawlessly. She finished second, merely fractions of a point behind the Russian gold medalist Irina Slutskaya. Michelle Kwan did not compete in the German or Canadian competitions.

In just three weeks, Tara had won three international medals! She must have felt as if she were living in a dream world. "To go from the U.S. to Canada to Paris to Germany in three weeks, and to be asked to compete against the world's best, was a little overwhelming," Tara admitted. "But once I was on the ice, I knew I was prepared. I knew I had the technical elements to do well. I just had to perform. Coach Callaghan has helped me peak at the right times, and I love the thrill of competing."

More than anything, Tara was looking forward to competing in the U.S. Figure Skating Championships in February. For figure-skating enthusiasts, no matter whether they were fans of "Leapin' Lipinski" or "Champion Kwan," that event in Nashville, Tennessee, promised to be quite a show.

TARA AND MICHELLE

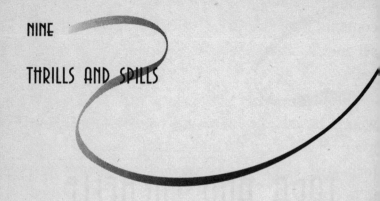

NINE

THRILLS AND SPILLS

Heading into the Nationals in February 1997, Tara and Michelle had different expectations. There was no doubt that Michelle was favored to win. She had captured a gold medal in eleven of her twelve previous competitions. She had even triumphed over the 1992 Olympic champion Kristi Yamaguchi in an Ultimate Four competition in January.

Tara was expecting to do well, too. But she wasn't expecting a first-place finish. "That's not a goal, to win," Coach Callaghan told a reporter before the Nationals. "She would have to skate her very best and Michelle would have to make some major mistakes. And Michelle's too good a competitor to do that. I would love to push for second. The big thing is to get back on the world team."

Tara was ready for this important competition with a new triple loop–triple loop combination jump. None of the older skaters had ever performed such a combination at the Nationals. But in her final days of practice before the big event, a funny thing happened. Tara lost a baby tooth!

Coach Callaghan wasn't exactly pleased when a newspaper printed the story about Tara's molar. He had worked too hard to make sure that Tara came across as an experienced, sophisticated skater. Now he was concerned that the judges would think of Tara as a little girl, baby teeth and all. But it was no use worrying now. There were lots of things Coach Callaghan could control, but Mother Nature was not one of them.

For the senior women skaters, competition at the Nationals began on Friday, February 14. It was Valentine's Day, and both Michelle and Tara had their hearts set on doing well in the short program. In the hours before the event, Tara was nervous. But a call from a world-famous gymnastics coach, Bela Karolyi, helped calm her down. Bela told her all she had to do was skate as well as she'd been skating in practice all season. Coach Callaghan echoed that advice, telling Tara to just "do her thing."

In a long-sleeved velvet outfit with a high lace collar, Tara skated a clean program to *Little Women*. She landed a triple Lutz–double loop combination and a triple flip—the toughest jumps of the night.

Michelle Kwan turned to Shakespearean tragedy for her short program. She skated the role of the good-hearted wife Desdemona, who was killed by her jealous husband, Othello. Michelle's combination of artistry and athleticism was as powerful as it had been all season. At the end of the night, she was ranked in first place. Tara was in second.

The next night Michelle put on her exquisite red costume, with its ornate golden sash, ready to perform her long program as the wife of an

Indian rajah. Her makeup was perfect, right down to the beauty mark that gave her the look of an authentic Indian princess.

Coach Carroll gave Michelle a little pep talk, telling her not to take any championship for granted. "You have to skate like you're taking the castle, not defending it," he told her.

Stepping on the ice, Michelle skated to the exotic music "Taj Mahal," by Fikret Amirov. She landed her second most difficult element: a triple Lutz–double toe loop combination. Then she moved straight into a planned triple toe–triple toe combination. She landed the first triple toe without a problem, but doubled the second and fell, right on her backside.

The audience was stunned. And so was Michelle. "I was standing up, then I was on the ice, and it was, like, 'What happened?'"

Michelle scrambled back to her feet and kept going, just as Coach Carroll had trained her to do. Whenever she had fallen in practice, Coach Carroll had made her get up and keep skating as if nothing had happened.

"If you miss something or trip on something

unexpectedly, that may be the only time in your life you get the opportunity to practice how you recover at that instant in the program," Carroll had once said. "If you let that opportunity go by, then you have not practiced that possibility of something happening."

Something had indeed happened to Michelle. Panicked, she stumbled badly on the next jump— a triple flip. "I was afraid of something," Michelle later said. "It was like a monster, and I was eaten by the monster."

To the crowd's dismay, Michelle attempted a triple loop and fell again. By now, the fans seemed to sense she needed help, so they began clapping for the champion, encouraging her to keep going. Their cheering seemed to give Michelle the strength to finish her program.

Backstage at the Nashville Arena, Tara Lipinski was busy adjusting her costume. "I was the next one on, so I had to retie my skates and get ready to go," she said. "I didn't have time to think, 'Oh, she didn't skate well. I have to win.' I just had to be confident and pretend it was a practice."

That's exactly what Tara did. She skated as well as she had in practice all week. Without a single mistake, she landed one perfect triple jump after another. The crowd roared its approval when she performed her historic triple loop–triple loop combination. And they didn't stop cheering until long after the flying camel she saved for the end.

Sitting in the "Kiss and Cry" area with her coach, Tara was the picture of youthful enthusiasm. "I'm on a different wavelength. Something high," she said. When her scores were announced, Tara let out a scream that seemed loud enough to rattle TV sets across the country. At fourteen, she had become the youngest champion in the history of the Nationals!

"Winning was a surprise," she told a reporter. "At first I was in shock, and for the rest of the night I acted all regular, but when I woke up the next day, I was like, 'Oh, my gosh. I can't believe it.'"

Coach Callaghan was just as surprised as Tara. But he was confident that Tara could handle her sudden victory. "I think Tara is bright enough to accept that she had a great night and the champion had an off night," Callaghan told the press.

What had caused the champion's "off night"? There were lots of different theories. Maybe Michelle was having trouble adjusting to her changing body. Maybe she'd become too cautious. Maybe she'd won so many competitions that she'd lost her competitive edge.

After Nashville, Michelle returned to the calm of Lake Arrowhead, no doubt hoping to find the source of her problem and fix it. Tara, by contrast, took a triple leap into the media spotlight.

From *Good Morning America* to *People* magazine, Tara's smile was everywhere. You could even find it on the Internet. Within hours of Tara's victory at the Nationals, her agent, Mike Burg, announced that Tara had her own web page. The page, called "Tara's Place," was filled with pictures, press releases, and even a feature called "Tara's Diary."

"I've got to tell you about the week *after* the

Nationals," Tara wrote in her on-line diary. "The trip to New York, the morning news shows, David Letterman, but I've got a ton of homework and I've got to get up early tomorrow for practice."

Yes, even the new national champion had to do her homework, get to bed on time, and practice, practice, practice. After all, the 1997 World Figure Skating Championships were coming up. Suddenly, it seemed, anything was possible for Tara Lipinski and Michelle Kwan.

TEN

THE ROAD TO THE WORLDS

"Tara's Place" on the Internet was by no means the *only* place for skating fans to visit. Over the years, Michelle Kwan had also developed a loyal following on-line. And after the Nationals, Michelle's cyberfans couldn't get to their computers fast enough to let Michelle know they were still one hundred percent behind her.

One fan told her to focus on the positive things in her life, such as her wonderful family and loyal fans. Others told Michelle that she'd accomplished more in her young life than many people would in a whole lifetime. Other fans seemed awed by Michelle's grace and dignity in a difficult situation. Everyone wanted Michelle to know how much they admired her, both as a champion skater and as a person.

But was her disastrous performance in Nashville just one stumble for Michelle? Or was her winning streak over for good? No one could know for certain. Yet Michelle would not have to wait until the World Championships to find out. Just two weeks after the Nationals, Michelle and Tara were back for a rematch at the Skate International Championship Finals in Ontario.

Both girls welcomed the opportunity to skate at Copps Coliseum—the largest arena in eastern Canada. Tara was excited to be competing as the new national champion. "The more performances you do," she said, "the more confidence you gain."

Michelle said she had put the memories of her Nationals performance behind her. "My confidence is fine," she told reporters. "At the Nationals, it was like God telling me to appreciate what you have." Now she was ready to move on.

At least she thought she was. When Michelle appeared on the ice for her short program, dressed in a black velvet skating outfit, she was her usual picture of elegance and grace. "That fear of what could happen isn't there because she *knows* what could happen," Coach Carroll explained. Unfortunately, it happened again. Michelle stumbled badly.

Tara, by contrast, soared through her short program, smiling and spinning to the upbeat soundtrack from *Little Women*. The rivalry between Tara and Michelle was heating up. Everyone in the audience could feel it. This wasn't going to deteriorate into a personality conflict off the ice, like the infamous battle between Tonya Harding and Nancy Kerrigan. This rivalry promised to be a thrilling competition on the ice between two totally dedicated, extremely talented young skaters.

The long program was broadcast on national television, adding to the pressure and the excitement. Tara skated fifth, right before Michelle. Seconds into her performance, Tara stumbled on a double axel, nearly colliding with the side-boards. But she caught herself in time, regained her balance, and went on to finish with her usual flourish.

Michelle's performance was the opposite of Tara's. Where Tara's start had been shaky, Michelle's start was solid. Tara's style had been light and airy, Michelle's was dramatic and exotic. But midway through her program, Michelle stumbled on a triple Lutz, struggled, and fell again.

Neither girl had a perfect night. And their scores reflected that fact. By the slimmest of margins—one-tenth of a point—Tara won the show-down and the gold medal.

There was no screaming this time. "This was nice and more experience for me," Tara said matter-of-factly. "So when I go to the Worlds, I'll have more confidence in myself because I've done it and this was a good warmup."

ELEVEN

THE YOUNGEST CHAMPION

Because of her age, Tara Lipinski nearly missed the chance to compete in the 1997 World Figure Skating Championships in Lausanne, Switzerland. Under the new rules, skaters had to be fifteen years old by the previous July before they would be allowed to compete at the Worlds or in the Olympics. Tara would not turn fifteen until the following June, three months *after* the World Championships.

Technically, fourteen-year-old Tara was ineligible for the 1997 Worlds. But skating officials decided to make an exception for her. Tara had already competed in the 1996 Worlds at the age of thirteen, so it didn't seem fair to suddenly decide she couldn't compete again at the age of fourteen.

Of course, that meant that if Tara were to win at the Worlds, she would be guaranteed a spot in skating history. Since no one younger than Tara would ever be allowed to compete, she would always have the distinction of being the youngest world champion!

The last time a fourteen-year-old skater had won the world title was back in 1927. Sonja Henie, a beautiful skater from Norway, was fourteen years and ten months old when she became the world champion. Tara would be fourteen years and nine months old if she won—one month younger than Sonja!

But even if Tara were to become the youngest world champion, Sonja Henie would always have her own place in history. That's because, after winning her first world title in 1927, Sonja went on to win that same title *ten* years in a row! She also won Olympic gold medals in 1928, 1932, and 1936.

Was Tara thinking about beating Sonja Henie's world record as she packed her suitcases for Switzerland? Apparently not. At a news conference in Lausanne just before the championship, reporters discovered that Tara didn't even seem to know about Sonja Henie's age record at the Worlds. Coach Callaghan gave her a quick history lesson.

When it finally came time for Tara to perform her short program, she could not afford to think about *any* skater's past history at the Worlds, especially her own. It was just a year ago that she had stumbled her way through her disastrous short program and finished in twenty-third place. Tara could not allow history to repeat itself!

She didn't have to worry. As the soundtrack from *Little Women* wafted through the arena, Tara launched into her short program. Her skating was crisp and clean, packed with all the spins, spirals, and leaps that she had perfected in the past year. She had a slight problem on her triple flip, barely making it off the ground. Her technical marks were lower than usual, but still high enough to put her in the lead.

Soon it was Michelle's turn. Would she be able to shake the monster that had swallowed her confidence at the Nationals? It was time to find out.

Michelle's opening spiral was a portrait in grace. But as she approached her triple Lutz, the monster reappeared. Michelle "stepped out" of her jump, meaning she didn't land it correctly. She turned and recovered quickly enough to pull off a double toe combination. But the damage had been done. She finished in fourth place.

Michelle seemed to be fighting back tears as she talked about her failed triple Lutz to reporters. "It makes me so mad," she said. "It's just one thing—out of so many—that I missed, but it's the one that counts the most."

It's easy to understand why Michelle was so upset. She had done hundreds of perfect triple Lutzes throughout the year. But on the one that counted—the one where the judges were watching—she had made a mistake.

Michelle had to remind herself that, in the grand scheme of things, a missed triple Lutz was not the end of the world. A sudden tragedy at the Worlds helped her put everything in perspective.

One of the most respected coaches in the world—Carlo Fassi—had a heart attack and died in Lausanne. His death was a terrible loss for his wife, Christa, who was also a coach. And it was a sad moment for all of the skaters Carlo Fassi had coached through the years, including Olympic stars Peggy Fleming and Dorothy Hamill.

Michelle had known Carlo Fassi through the Ice Castle training center. Fassi had come to the '97 Worlds as Nicole Bobek's latest coach. Like all the other coaches who had worked with Nicole before him, Carlo Fassi had been trying to add some stability to her skating career.

As Coach Fassi lay dying, he asked his wife, Christa, to give Nicole the strength and support she needed to finish the competition.

The night of the long program was filled with mixed emotions for all the skaters who had known Carlo Fassi. In the air, there was the usual excitement of the event. But there was also a real sense of loss.

Nicole skated her long program out of respect for Carlo Fassi. As might be expected, she had a hard time concentrating on her routine. She stumbled several times and struggled repeatedly as her eyes filled with tears. At the end of her performance, Nicole fell to her knees in an emotional tribute to her former coach.

When it was Tara's turn to skate her long program, she knew she had to stay focused. "That day," she wrote in her on-line diary, "I tried to act as if it were just another day. I went to a little restaurant and had some pizza, and then went back to my hotel room and just vegged out. I skated late that afternoon, and really, the hardest part was after I skated—waiting! Once I stepped onto the ice, I felt better. With each jump I landed, I gained more confidence. By the end of the program, I knew I had skated my best, and I was so happy with myself."

The hard part indeed came after Tara's performance. She had to wait almost an hour to find out if she'd won the world title. That's because several other skaters after Tara still had to perform their long programs, including Michelle Kwan.

Michelle wanted desperately to do well in her long program. She had to put all of her past disappointments out of her mind. In the moments before she took to the ice, she thought about Carlo Fassi and another legendary skater—Scott Hamilton.

Scott had always been a role model for Michelle. He had recently been diagnosed with cancer. Now he was going to have to wage a battle against the disease.

Michelle was thankful that this skating competition, no matter how important it seemed to her, was not about life or death. *This is just an event*, she told herself as she skated out on the ice. If she didn't win, nothing horrible would happen. She'd have another chance.

Calm and confident, Michelle skated like the old Michelle. Once again she was the exotic Indian princess, skating artistically, jumping smoothly. At the end of her routine, the crowd roared its approval. They were happy to see this champion skater back in control.

But the event still wasn't over. Tara's waiting game continued. And now Michelle had to wait too, as eighteen-year-old Irina Slutskaya of Russia performed her long program. During practice that day, Irina had fallen and crashed into the sideboards. At the last minute, she decided to skip a triple Salchow she had planned in her program.

Finally, it was time to decide who had won.

When the scores were added up, Michelle Kwan had actually won the long program. But that victory wasn't enough to make up for her fourth-place finish in the short program. Tara Lipinski was declared the winner—the youngest woman ever to capture the world championship. Michelle took the silver medal. And Vanessa Gusmeroli of France received the bronze.

The rivalry between Tara and Michelle had brought out the best in both skaters. It had challenged Michelle, tested her will, and pushed her to become an even stronger skater. It had given

Tara an opportunity to show the world that her love for skating was as genuine as her smile.

But in the end, the real winners were the fans. They knew they could look forward to many more brilliant performances from Tara Lipinski *and* Michelle Kwan in the years ahead.

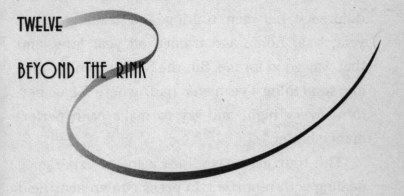

TWELVE

BEYOND THE RINK

After the World Championships, both Tara and Michelle spent the spring touring the country. Michelle had been on tour before, so she knew what to expect. But for Tara, being the star attraction on a national tour was a new experience. So were the big paychecks, the crowds, and the constant traveling. She and her mother would wake up in one hotel room in one city. And the next morning, they'd wake up in a different hotel room in a different city.

Going on tour can be an exhausting experience. But it can also be an exciting break from training. On one of her early tour stops in Providence, Rhode Island, Tara talked about the difference between touring and training. "Last year, I sat home and trained all year long, and that was good for me. But the tour is going to give me something I've never had, where I can perform every night and try to make each performance better."

The tour also gave Tara a lot of experience dealing with reporters. In press conferences held before each performance, reporters constantly asked Tara about the problems of being a young superstar.

"I think that whatever age you're at, if you can actually do what everyone else is doing and you're up to their level, then I don't understand why it would be a problem," Tara replied. "I work just as hard as everyone else to get to that level."

Like Tara, Michelle also worked hard on tour, making sure to put all her energy into each nightly show. She had little respect for the skaters who goofed off on tour. "I'm always pretending it's the Olympics," Michelle once said about touring.

"Some skaters say: 'It's only a show. I can fall all over the place and still get paid.' What attitude is that?"

Michelle traveled with her mother, and often her father joined them. Mr. Kwan had retired early from his job at Pacific Bell to help Michelle prepare for the Olympics and to spend more time with his two other children, Karen and Ronnie.

Of course, Michelle and Tara had to find the time to keep up on their schoolwork, even though they were on tour. That meant reading on buses and planes, backstage, and in hotel rooms—wherever they could find a quiet place to concentrate.

What about the future? Both Tara and Michelle are A students, and they both plan on going to college. "I'm keeping my fingers crossed," Tara's mother once said, "because my dream is for her to go to one of the best colleges in the country."

Michelle is even more specific about her college dreams. She has often said that after the Olympics, she would like to go to Harvard

University. And after that, she might even want to go to law school.

Would college mean the end of Michelle's skating career? Not necessarily. Michelle's older sister, Karen, has managed to combine skating with a college education at Boston University. "I thought it was best for me, but I didn't realize how difficult it was until I got into it," Karen told a reporter during her freshman year. "Now I know what I've gotten myself into."

Karen always makes up for the classes she misses when she competes in skating events around the world. Yet she knows it would be harder for Michelle to continue skating while in college. Karen is the first to admit that her little sister has always been under more pressure to succeed.

"I think it's a lot harder for Michelle than it is for me," Karen once told a reporter. "Because when she walks into a rink, people know who she is, and she has to be perfect at all times. And that's just not human."

Both Michelle and Tara are working hard to

find the right balance in their lives. They want to balance their skating with their studies. They want to be world-famous skaters, but there are days they'd also just like to be treated like normal teenagers.

Tara's mother says she tries to make time for Tara to be a typical kid. "She works hard all week," Mrs. Lipinski once said, "but come Friday night, the sleepover begins, she browses nonstop at the mall, talks nonstop on the phone." Of course, there's not a lot of time for sleepovers on tour. But the Lipinskis say they often let Tara take a friend on her travels, just so she doesn't miss out on the joy of friendship.

Friends are important to Michelle, too. Once, when Michelle was fourteen, a reporter asked her what she'd do if she had two extra hours in the day. "I would talk with friends," she said. "That's what my fun time is, talking with friends and family."

When Michelle was sixteen, she discovered another fun way to spend time with friends—driving in her own car! But it took her a little longer than usual to get her license. The first time she took her driver's test, she failed!

"I was so nervous," Michelle said. "I was sweating, and my hands were, like, gripping the wheel. I did really bad. I mean, oh, yuck."

Michelle didn't pass her test because she couldn't do what's called a three-point turn. The same girl who could do triple axels on the ice couldn't turn a car around in three simple steps! It was a funny twist of fate. But Michelle's father reminded her that driving was serious business. Mr. Kwan even made Michelle write a thank-you note to the instructor who had tested her, saying she was grateful for the lesson in car safety.

After failing her test the first time, Michelle practiced her driving with the same determination that she practiced her skating. And when she took the test a second time, she passed. Michelle rewarded herself by buying a gold-colored Jeep. Now there are days when she looks like a typical teenager around Lake Arrowhead, hopping in her Jeep and driving to the local waffle shop. But her eating habits give her away. She'll order a plain bran waffle, with the whipped cream on the side. She also eats plenty of pasta and vegetables and fish, but never fried food.

Staying in shape. Giving up time with your friends. Spending most of your waking hours at an ice rink. Squeezing in your schoolwork between competitions and exhibitions. It's not a normal life. But it's the life that Tara and Michelle have chosen.

"I wouldn't want to have the same life that everyone has," Tara said after winning the World Championships. "I love my life. Skating is what I do."

"I want to be a legend, like Dorothy Hamill and Peggy Fleming," Michelle said a year before the Olympics. "I want to leave a little mark. What am I going to do if I don't win the Olympics? I guess I'd be disappointed. But you have to learn to cope and be happy and enjoy life. A lot of things aren't going to go your way."

Michelle and Tara have every reason to be happy, no matter who ends up with more

Olympic gold medals. They've already won the respect of their fans. And with all their hard work, sacrifices, and talent, these two world champions have added a special shine to the sport of figure skating—a shine far brighter than gold.

OLYMPIC GOLD MEDALISTS
FIGURE SKATING—WOMEN'S SINGLES

1908	Madge Syers, Great Britain
1920	Magda Julin-Maurey, Sweden
1924	Herma von Szabo-Planck, Austria
1928	Sonja Henie, Norway
1932	Sonja Henie, Norway
1936	Sonja Henie, Norway
1948	Barbara Ann Scott, Canada
1952	Jeanette Altwegg, Great Britain
1956	Tenley Albright, U.S.
1960	Carol Heiss, U.S.
1964	Sjoukje Dijkstra, Netherlands
1968	Peggy Fleming, U.S.
1972	Beatrix Schuba, Austria
1976	Dorothy Hamill, U.S.
1980	Anett Poetzsch, E. Germany
1984	Katarina Witt, E. Germany
1988	Katarina Witt, E. Germany
1992	Kristi Yamaguchi, U.S.
1994	Oksana Baiul, Ukraine
1998	?

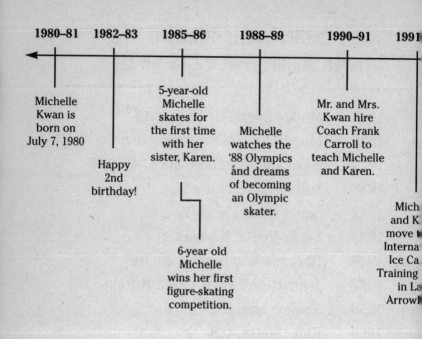

| 1980–81 | 1982–83 | 1985–86 | 1988–89 | 1990–91 | 1991 |

Michelle Kwan is born on July 7, 1980

Happy 2nd birthday!

5-year-old Michelle skates for the first time with her sister, Karen.

6-year old Michelle wins her first figure-skating competition.

Michelle watches the '88 Olympics and dreams of becoming an Olympic skater.

Mr. and Mrs. Kwan hire Coach Frank Carroll to teach Michelle and Karen.

Mich and K move Interna Ice Ca Training in La Arrowh

MICHELLE KWAN
TIME LINE

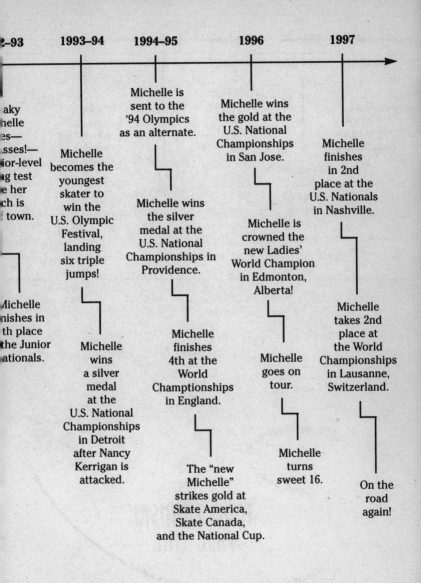

2–93 | **1993–94** | **1994–95** | **1996** | **1997**

...aky
...helle
...sses!—
...ior-level
...g test
...e her
...ch is
... town.

Michelle becomes the youngest skater to win the U.S. Olympic Festival, landing six triple jumps!

Michelle is sent to the '94 Olympics as an alternate.

Michelle wins the gold at the U.S. National Championships in San Jose.

Michelle finishes in 2nd place at the U.S. Nationals in Nashville.

Michelle wins the silver medal at the U.S. National Championships in Providence.

Michelle is crowned the new Ladies' World Champion in Edmonton, Alberta!

...Michelle
...nishes in
...th place
...the Junior
...ationals.

Michelle wins a silver medal at the U.S. National Championships in Detroit after Nancy Kerrigan is attacked.

Michelle finishes 4th at the World Champtionships in England.

Michelle goes on tour.

Michelle takes 2nd place at the World Championships in Lausanne, Switzerland.

The "new Michelle" strikes gold at Skate America, Skate Canada, and the National Cup.

Michelle turns sweet 16.

On the road again!

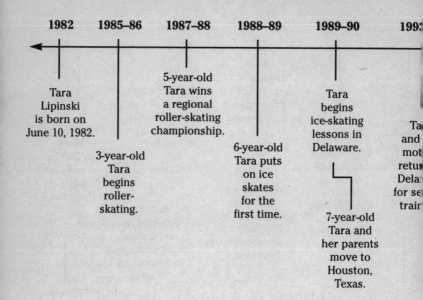

1982

Tara Lipinski is born on June 10, 1982.

1985–86

3-year-old Tara begins roller-skating.

1987–88

5-year-old Tara wins a regional roller-skating championship.

1988–89

6-year-old Tara puts on ice skates for the first time.

1989–90

Tara begins ice-skating lessons in Delaware.

7-year-old Tara and her parents move to Houston, Texas.

199

Ta and mot retu Dela for se train

TARA LIPINSKI
TIME LINE

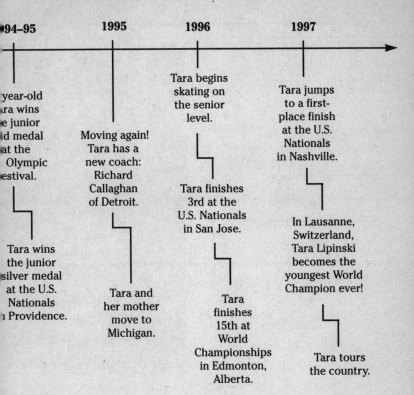

1994–95

year-old
[Ta]ra wins
[th]e junior
[go]ld medal
[at] the
[ ] Olympic
[F]estival.

Tara wins
the junior
[ ]silver medal
at the U.S.
Nationals
[i]n Providence.

1995

Moving again!
Tara has a
new coach:
Richard
Callaghan
of Detroit.

Tara and
her mother
move to
Michigan.

1996

Tara begins
skating on
the senior
level.

Tara finishes
3rd at the
U.S. Nationals
in San Jose.

Tara
finishes
15th at
World
Championships
in Edmonton,
Alberta.

1997

Tara jumps
to a first-
place finish
at the U.S.
Nationals
in Nashville.

In Lausanne,
Switzerland,
Tara Lipinski
becomes the
youngest World
Champion ever!

Tara tours
the country.